HOMEGROWN

SUBHADRA HODIGERE

To all the life I've seen bloom around me

Contents

Contents

Foreword

Homegrown. What does it mean to be homegrown? Was I grown on the ground that you cultivated? I am a result of your seed? Am I simply another version of you, with no claims to authenticity and identity. What am I, if I am home grown

Am I Indian? Where my passport says otherwise. What courses through my veins- the blood of some strong ancestor or one too weak to counter the pain. Did they live in their comfortable silence, did they live in peace? Did the roles assigned to them at birth shield them from reality?

Am I homegrown like the weeds in your garden? Stinging like the nettles you are afraid to cut, or weak like the dandelions easily trampled. My rage feels so calamitous but my being feels just as weak. Who stares back at me, when I look inside that mirror. Am I mere reverberations of body and flesh?

Am I homegrown or am I an alien

Preface

In august 2021, I was consumed by deep and seemingly inescapable rage and anguish. From that pain, I engendered my book 'Labyrinth'. Despite being a product of my very being, I know look back and that work and find a sense of resentment and distaste. My words were unfinished, my sentences unpunctuation, unexplained and incomplete. The words came from a place of revenge rather than unerstanding. I was hell bent on proving the world wrong; wrong that it cast me aside and wrote me off as a no good. Today, I have faced rejection and hardship far past what I had known 6 months ago. Today, I come to myself with peace. Or at the very least, an effort of peace and understanding. Compared to the poems of labyrinth, these are mere infants, written only in the last 6 months. Yet, they contain worlds beond what my words once did then.

here in the coming years to see you grow, to see you change and sprout new leaves like the ivy that grows beside our parent's balcony. There's truly no force on this planet that compares to your sharp mind and witty tongue. You know more than me, so any advice I give is entirely futile. But know, that I love you very dearly.

I'd like to thank all my friends, Isha, Tamanna, Adi, Diya, Aarushi, Cathy and many more. You've again shown me that love isn't limited.

To my teachers, every single one of them. A special thanks to Vineetha ma'am, the first teacher that found potential in me when I couldn't recognize even a speck of it. Your continued belief in me since the age of 12 gave me the courage to continue writing and growing

And finally, to Michelle Zauner and Ocean Vuong. I'm about 100% you'll never find their book, but on the off chance that you do. Your music and books held me and comforted me in ways I can't fathom into words. In your sentences and phrases I found parts of myself as I silently cried and laughed on crammed metros and buses. Thank you.

Prologue

"Why see the world, when you got the beach?"

- Frank Ocean.

"You Need To Go To War
To Find Material To Sing"

- Florence + the machine

I hate how much of me

Is in my writing

My words and sentences

Beginning with the selfish I

Ending with me

How can I write

So much,

Lines upon lines

About a person I don't even know

I contemplate

Over and over

Of what the world thinks of me

To no response

No respite

To these growing tremors

It seems every time I've come to a conclusion

Or some grand revelation

It's broken and discarded

New or unseen facets of my being

Growing out like the bud

That tears out of a hydra

New life they say

New life shouldn't bring such pain,

Should it?

Sunlight seeps through

fitting through the smallest of cracks and breaks

across the pavement and into the walls

where it may reach me

I see it,

in all its golden glory,

waxing and waning upon the hardwood buildings and plaster of Paris roofs

Far across from where I stand

Panels are lit ablaze,

But- They are undying

Catching fire every night and day-

Blinding my sight

Piercing my eyes-

Yet, I remain looking

Aware of the consequences, unafraid

I wonder aloud, as my gazes scream in pain

Oh, gods of the mighty sun

Those that stand tall above

Why must such beauty cause me pain?

Seldom do they respond,

moving about in despondence

I am but a mere mortal

A sheep under their control

This fire gives you life, they say

And with life, must come pain.

Soon, winter will be here

and all will be dead and gone.

The children of a spring shall fade

and the newly fallen autumn leaves shall wither away

a ground ever so rigid,

from which no plant can fathom to grow

With an air so frigid and old,

tiresome from its lengthy travels across the blood red fields

and black laden plateaus

It has arrived to take us with its misery

fogging up early morning glory,

so, school children may stand shiver in its embrace

Thus, the winter will have arrived

and I shall feel a pang of happiness in my chest

For the uncanny friendship

That it shares with me

I fell in love

with the skylines and neon lights

the first time i saw them

I knew I was home

the iridescent glow of ultraviolence

that hit my plastic glasses night after night

louder than the screams of my wobbly knees

and blistering feet

each crack on the pavement seemed a tributary

of this undying city

each nook and cranny a new adventure

somewhere along the line,

the computer click of my camera

found my soul and laid still

those stills in my mind

I think of them day after day

night after night

in a city that I call my home

but is far from my own

where no neon lights shine

and the shutters and windows go out,

almost as swiftly as the age-old sun

In those quiet nights,

in those dark lights

I long and pine for the city that became home

When I dive into that abyss

It makes no sense to me

That my world has turned crystal

Everything is a deep blue

Maybe there

Where all sound dare not reach

Where light is a mere figment of my imagination

My loud mind will know some peace

The thoughts that constantly echo

Will fail to reverberate through my ears

And my brows,

In their perpetual stressful state

Will untangle, and rest easy

These muscles and bones

Tired from their harsh encounters

Wondering what lead them to that very cart

Slowly, they slip from my mind

As something else,

More important, more dire

Occupies my mind

And so I go on

Seeing and being seen

In the morning

I move forward,

In the evening

I move back,

A routine I've crafted for myself

Somedays I am tiresome

Others I feel nothing

Today,

I felt the rain on my skin

While the sun stood above head

The streets didn't turn grey

As they usually do

But they remained dotted with raindrops

And within me

A happiness unfurled slowly

As the jasmine flowers opened

Greeting the sweet summer rain

And the petrichor prepared itself for arrival

Staring deep into my eyes

I saw a dog,

One so like own brother

Mismatched flaps for ears

He stared at me with intent

Slowly,

Taking out a packet of biscuits

Be greeted me with a keen wag of his tail

As his comrade came out from the shadows

I said my goodbye

But he didn't follow me

An unsaid agreement

To give and receive love

From strangers on rainy days

It is at these moments

That I'm reminded why I love this city

And these tar streets

When I was 14

You sent me a playlist

It was nearing 3 AM

And we would both be sleep deprived

On yellow and green buses the next day

Awake at that unfathomable hour

You said I'd probably like this music

I sent you one back,

Saying the exact same

Words were difficult

So we sat in silence during lunch

Eating box bound lunches

Occasionally passing a few words

At bare daybreak

With my string of earphones plugged

I heard the strain

Of Gerard way's voice

I heard words

I never knew I needed

To hear or to say

I heard myself echoing through

Slowly I learnt about the northern downpour

Sending all its love

All of these things

They make me who I am

Laughing over two overgrown british men

And missing sweat dripping PE classes

We stuck together

And you held me above the growing water

There are a million things

I wish I had told you in the last four years

That you were here

But now you are a million miles away

So I write you this poem

Not as a final goodbye

But just,

Something to remember me by

My grandmother,

Ritualistic and precise in her practices

Stands in front of me

A single red chili in her hand

She drags in the air

Over and over,

In circumference around me

To protect me

There's a single red chili

Set ablaze on an open stove top

She says, peacefully

That if my throat does burn

And broken coughing doesn't escape me

I have been seen

Seen as beautiful,

Peculiar, I furrow my brows

I've seen this practice

Through the years

Done on birthdays

And to wish someone goodbye

But never out of the blue,

Never so sudden

She sees me as beautiful,

And I find it hard to believe

Perhaps it's her affection,

Covering what is reality

But in that moment

One filled with her infinite love

I see myself as she sees me

For beauty

Something I never thought I would be

Beauty,

Such a novel, romantic idea

It isn't to be pretty

But to be something beyond aesthetic

Complex, beauty isn't linear

And I find myself

Standing on granite tiles

To be similar

To the ocean, pearly and violent

Stagnant and immortal

Brief and ever long

A creature of beauty

Emptiness

There is no void,

No great expense-

ahead of me

But I sense emptiness

So immense, so overwhelming

It threatens to drown me

Silence me

Blank pages

Lines beyond lines

Printed using indifferent molds

To become my nemesis

Hovering a little above

The nip of a newly filled pen

Threatens to drip

And bleed through the barren paper

Better still,

Than the words

That stop at my throat

Choking me out,

Leaving me dry

There is so much I wish to say

A tumtulous, loud universe in my mind

But I can't bring myself

To find the words

Instead,

I sit in silence

And stare blankly ahead

Hoping they'll finally

Bloom from their unmanifest shells

And take on my form

Interlude

It was as I was becoming cognitive about my own identity that I began to read about identity. I found that writers, poets, artists all circled around this idea. What does it mean to be? Who are we? What are we?

In searching for my own identity, I often got lost, misguided or confused. But those aren't weaknesses, paradoxically they allowed me to cultivate the being I am today. I'm still far from fully informed about my existence, but each day I find another puzzle piece added to the maze that constitutes me. There are lines and alleyways that soon will disappear. They will become unimportant in my personhood for the moment. However, not for a lifetime

Interestingly, in my venture into literature about such an ambivalent subject, I came across a theory put forward by Mead. He theorised that community, the way one interacts with those around creates the centralised "me". Yet, it is the individual and active perception of this "me" that constitutes "I"- how you see yourself. It was at this moment that I realised, to be fully actualized one had to surround themselves with love. It is important that those near are able to see the reality of their comrade rather than a glamorised or reduced individual.

We grow to be our parent's children

Not so dissimilar

We find parts of ourselves in them

And they in us,

Funny isn't it

We seem to inherit the worst of them

Sharing their rage or misery

Echoing words long gone

Or unsaid

We vye for their love

Hoping to be enough

Each cut-wound scar,

A reminder of how we simply aren't enough

This is self-infliction

An unspoken and unexplainable need

Need to make you proud

Need to make you happy

You've never asked much of me

So I try,

Day and day out

To be the child you wanted

But I often fail

If I am all that you are

Does that make my name yours too?

I carry pieces of you

Will that make you another version of you

When I grow older

And my childish disposition

Holds me no more

Equal parts

White milk and clear water

You always preferred your chai

In that very consistency

You never put sugar into the kettle

Instead scooping up the sweet grains

And mixing the brown tinted liquid

Still emanating steam

You like your coffee strong

Filling half the glass

In hourlong steeped decoction

And the other with cold milk

Only the microwave's magnetism could warm it

Whilst the heaped scoops of jaggery slowly melt away

You drink in complete silence

As the morning breeze wades slowly about you

Dipping bakery baked biscuits

And feeding hungry dogs

I don't know the secrets

Held tightly behind those iron filled

Flood gates, guarded by the fiercest of soldiers

But I know how you take your tea

And your coffee

For me,

That's enough

Crying in the blue bus

I sit on blue seats

As a blue floor runs alongside me

My blue pants cling to my legs

And my eyes spill blue tears

The sun around me is blazing

The yellow auto and bus stands

They want me to be happy

How can I

When my mind is haywire

And my body will not let me rest

The sun high above

Is cruel until no one attempts to compete

I hate myself

I curse aimlessly under my breathe

No longer is summer that vision of relief

Instead, I’ve carried my misery

I'm bone tired

For 4 years I’ve known no rest

Pushing away those I love

For a goal I never did meet

I simply wasn’t enough

My pious pain too futile

My tears have stopped

But my throat longs to cry

I let my silent agony burst through me

As a cry on this blue bus

Yellow house

Yellow house lost on the horizon

Yellow house, too quick to say goodbye

Yellow house, why do you hurt me so

Why does my heart quench?

And cry out in misery

I've seen you only but once

Your body draped by a thin veil of black

I see your tear-stricken eyes

Yellow house,

Oh, my dear yellow house

Has the world been cruel to you?

Have you sustained years of pain?

Yellow house

Why do I love you so?

My youth has failed me

I don't know how to live

A state of perpetual horror

Resides in me

Lately, I've been stumbling

Over and over

Falling over rocky roads

They said it would become easier

But it hasn't

If anything, its harder

Going through the motions

With ambivalent horror

Scarred knees

And bruised elbows

I can't look at myself in the mirror

Because I don't know who stares at me

Do I like myself today?

Or will I writhe away in pain

It seems so much easier

To run and hide

Then there will be no more stumbling

My bruised misery will depart

With no misery

When my anguish is long gone

What will be left of me?

When the Sakura falls

The city lanes are shrouded

In pale pink disposition

Too many to count

The bone bare branches

Now move in heart heavy tremulous

Stooping lower and lower

Until the season has said its last goodbye

Kissing the roads of fire

With all its honesty and integrity

Promising to return

There will be another season soon

Another lover to caress the mud and tear streets

Until then,

The Sakura will bloom and fall

Filling the ever-grey skies

With fleeting beauty

It isn’t fair

That we must be the saviours of the broken

The beaten

And the damned

If we haven’t left them in that sorry state

Why must we must we fight

To save the world that you’ve so cruelly destroyed

They always say

The perpetrator must take responsibility

But that is far from the truth

Isn’t it

It’s always that clueless witness

That is left with perfidy

From those closest or even dearest

Sweating from the ever-rising heat

Do you think the water will drown us out?

Do you think the parched will turned famished?

Only to vanish with a trace

From the growing power and rage

Trapped inside this pierced firmament

Of course, you don't

If you truly did

Then you'd do something

Except sign futile pieces of paper

Simply discarded or tucked away

Amongst your growing stack

Of unfilled promises

And wide-eyed lies

Afterall,

When the green bills trickle in

And another steely white yacht

Or hold statue is paid for

Who cares about the world?

That you won't live in

There are some houses that I pass

Too worn by time

Their once stellar painted exteriors

Now withering away

From months of rain and heat

Right next

There are those new houses

Newly painted, dripping with acetone

And still drying hues

Their strokes hidden behind layers

Layers and layers

Of indifference

One of the seldom examples

Of paint becoming simply a cover,

Not a medium

Distaste and disregard

It pays off, to be careless

Or is it to not care,

They truly are far different things

It is only what is new,

What is shining

That attracts the hands

To reach out and grab it,

As if it is worthy of love

Time wears people down

But people wear time down

Sanding and dusting off

Until it is but a mere speckle

Is that 3 story house

The one embraced by the waves of time

Is it a speckle?

Is it brief, and forgotten

Or can it be reborn?

Vuong said words can create

But they can never regenerate

To paint over its lines

We futilely believe it's another chance

We will revive it,

Regenerate it, let it grow

Except we are killing it

And creating something new

Ironic isn't it,

How all art,

All that is new and hold

Is born of pain and death

I used to speak in the tongue of my mother

Or so I'm told

Before my mouth could grasp the syllables,

Slick like the top of hard-boiled eggs

A, E, I, O, U

I spoke in the words of my own

They were bent smooth,

Ricocheting with my childish disposition

The sound sh, a far off dream to pronounced

There were no goos and gahs

I seemed to have outgrown them far too soon

Instead, there were old songs

Kicked up in the unforgiving

And boring summer heat,

Far from a place I knew as my own

But it wasn't home

Truly, a blur with a cot and a roof

A shelter more than a home

Being with you both,

Took that lofty soft

So when you laughed in praise

And encouraged my naive tongue

I took it as victory,

As security of my home

And my own

Until I lost it all,

Picking up foreign letters and vowels

Discarding what was used and old

For some new shiny technology

I don't remember the moment I made the switch

But soon the slick vowels coursed through my veins

As if their whiteness my bleach my only darkening brown

And their class, their infinite wealth

Might treat me better

I, O, U

Is this what I owe you

To create in a language

So far from my own?

To struggle and confound myself

With broken clauses and sentences

Years after we departed

From a land across the 7 seas

Because even in the country

That is my own,

My words, The words that were given to me

As a toddler, wrapped in garbs and garlands of gold

Is seen as inept,

Unlearned, and lacking

For to speak in the coloniser's tongue

Is to hold a mark of prestige

And to speak in your own,

Is to accept the shameful truth

Of your supposed inferiority

One of the best things of my life

Was watching it go by

From the sidelines

I had a front row seat to everything

With gigantic 3D glasses

To finish the part

I saw the world move around me

The breeze pick up and die down

The seasons crashing and receding

I could feel life around

All its beauty

All its death

And mourn it while the world moved on

Maybe being stuck and sidelined

Isn't so sorrowful afterall

9 798887 045856

Printed by Libri Plureos GmbH in Hamburg, Germany